I0829849

GLAM SKANK

Vol. 01 Winter 2018

PATRICIA MANNING
Editor in Chief

Unison Music Group LLC.
Publisher

Managing Editor Bethany Taryeton • **Executive Editor** Bruce Witkin

Creative Director • Mitch Goodman

Director Photography:
Len Scapon

Contributing Photographers:
Suzanne Allison
David Kleeman
Millie Chan
Mitch Goodman
Rick O'Shea

Editorial:
Patricia Manning
Bethany Taryeton
Hugo First

Holiday Fashion Consultant:
Don Weenau

Holiday Fashion Assistant:
Aretha Holley

House Band:
Glam Skanks

Additional Contributors:
Phylis Steen · Jay Walker
Ed Emame · Joaquin Closet

Tailors/Costumes:
Preston Creases
Hugh Jass

Footwear Consultant:
Susan Shocks

Director Innovation:
Chi Chi Urbanair

Director Craft Service:
Sir. Irving Spoon

Craft Service Staff:
Tyra Meesu
Eureka Garlick
Russell Upsumgrub

Product Management:
Thought Squad

Communication:
Kurt Reply

Public Relations:
Bea Esser

Access Coordinator:
Doris Shutt

Administration:
Neil Down
Upton Leftus

Finance:
Max Stout
Lois Bidder

Reception:
Levon Holde

Security:
Barb Dwyer

BAD BITCHES

When Glam Skanks learned they were to support "The Adicts" for a couple Halloween shows, little did they know that Adicts front-man *Monkey* would take them out on the town for sushi and adventures...the start of a fantabulous friendship! Monkey is known for outrageous stage shows and even though the girls always kill it, they wanted make sure to slay the crowd, so they dressed as the infamous *Deadly Viper Assassination Squad.* Needless to say, the band was bloody brilliant! Big thanks to Monkey, the Adicts, their crew and House of Blues.

Millie Chan	Vannessa McNeil	Veronica Witkin	Jessica Goodwin
Bass/Vocals	Lead Vocal	Guitar/Vocals	Drums

T-Shirts
Stickers
GLAM SKANKS
GLAM SKANKS
Embroidered Patch
GLAM SKANKS
GLITTER CITY
Glitter City CD
Condoms
GLAM SKANKS
Buttons
GLAM SKANKS
@GLAMSKANKS
@Glamskanks
MERCH

COLOR

Patience
+
Practice
=
Perfection!

Photo: Suzanne Allison

Hair has always been one of the most important parts of any rock star look. From Little Richard and Jerry Lee Lewis, to heaps of hippie hair, to dagger-sharp Mohawks and Flock of Seagulls doo-don'ts, rock and roll style takes it from the top! Here is a quick look at what goes in to a radiant, rainbow doo.

MAKE SPACE for your tools and supplies, blast some Bowie and go for it! Patience and practice wins the day and experimentation is required to get what you are going for. What better pallet for crazy colors than your classy colored coiffure!

GREAT GLAM GLOW will require you to care for your hair, so remember to give plenty of time to heal from the beating that bleach brings. A fresh cut is best, so start with a style you like, as it will be some time before you trim your tenacious tresses.

A FUN FRIENDLY ASSISTANT will make the experience so much better! Hard to reach spots, and a "take-a-step-back" perspective do wonders for full coverage and straight lines.

BLEACH IS A BITCH but needed for vibrant colors. Dark hair takes several rounds of bleaching to get it right. Figure three times, with about ten days of non-stop conditioning in between each bleaching.

PETROLEUM JELLY IS YOUR FRIEND so use it generously on all exposed skin. You can apply conditioner to the hair you don't want dyed and your scalp. Grab the gloves and section off your hair. Mix the dye until it's smooth and paint it onto your bleached hair using downward strokes.

Use (gloved) fingers to work dye through each section of hair. When done, twist, clip and wait about an hour. Take at least 10 or 15 minutes to fully wash out the color and make sure that after you shampoo and condition, the water runs completely clear.

Patience + Practice = Perfection!

...A FUN FRIENDLY ASSISTANT
will make the experience so much better!

...Hard to Reach Spots
and a "take-a-step-back" perspective do
wonders for full coverage and straight lines.

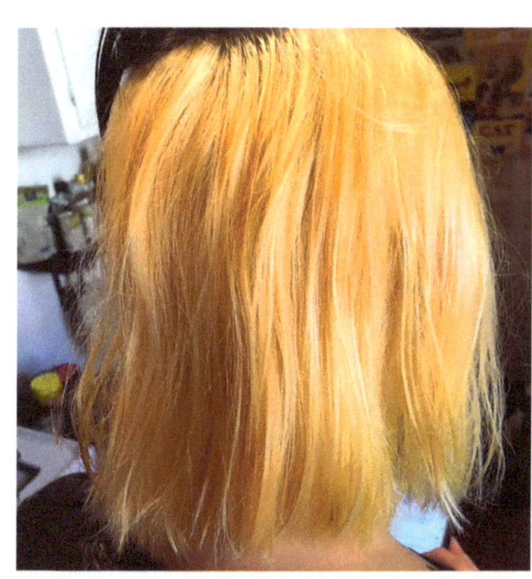

Glam GEAR

Text: Patricia Manning

Photos • Suzanne Allison

Here come the holy daze... As the seasons seem to change later and later, and we head towards an inevitable, permanent heatwave, the true indicator of seasonal change is dictated by the shit on the shelves in the stores; not the weather.

Sadly, since Halloween is no longer a reverent "harvest festival", but instead a costumed blood bath, last minute costumes are easy... Try a thrift store wedding dress lovingly splattered with red food coloring. Here's another very simple, dirt-cheap costume that anyone can make at home:

- Find large, plastic Trash Bag
- Cut a hole in bottom of the bag
- Poke head through hole in bag
- Pull bag over shoulders
- Cut arm holes according to size
- **45th U.S. President**

After Halloween is dead, the invitations for Thanksgiving, cocktail parties and other end of the year festivities find their way to your door. Now faced with a busy social calendar that will require *class* attire, it's time to plan for the parties! Try new things... mixing and matching clothes you already have with new items you purchase.

The haughty, high-priced, highbrow, holiday haberdasheries are always way too expensive and even Target and Ross can really add up. Instead, how bout gearing up with goodies from Goodwill! Thrift Stores are your best friends boys and girls (and everyone in between). Community closets are bursting at the seams with fabulous finery! You can find that fab formal for a fraction of the funds!

With a bit of creativity and little work, you can design your own "Glam Gear", suitable for any occasion. Show off "*your*" personal style by taking existing clothing and transforming it into your very own glad rags. Going through the racks of used garments, you might fall in love with a fabric or style, but bummer, there's neon green pipping and pockets. No worries! Cut up several items and marry them to create an awesome, new, completely original ensemble. Just think fashion ala Frankenstein!

It is always wise to "pay the price" for an awesome, "must-have" pair of boots, bag or something super special that is versatile and can be used often. However, amazing attire can be your own creation! Affordable one-of-a-kind outfits are fun to make and a great way build up a respectable, (original) wardrobe.

It is always wise to "pay the price" for an awesome, "must-have" pair of boots, bag or something super-special that is versatile and can be used often.

There are no Fashion Police...

If you plan to slice, slash and sew,
a basic sewing kit is in order.

Thrift store shopping is where it's at! Find thrift stores that have a lot of turn over. Salvation Army and Goodwill have so much stuff, they usually sell it super-cheap. Also, finding these stores in affluent neighborhoods can be a goldmine! One gals' trash is another's treasure. Garbage to glam!

And don't forget the many smaller, church, or community run thrift shops that are bound to have awesome antique attire! Old lady jewelry and jackets can be found at these fun, friendly establishments. Beware the boutiques! Don't overpay because a trendy shop has some super-cool, but over-priced, outfit on a vintage mannequin!

Always shop with friends! Not only does this guarantee that your treasure hunt is more exciting, (and safe!) a second pair of eyes is helpful. Always remember: There are NO Fashion Police. Just be YOU!

- Polyester Thread (basic colors)
- Scissors (large)
- Scissors (small)
- Seam Riper
- Pin Cushion
- Tape Measure
- Safety Pins
- Dressmaker Pins
- Hand Needles
- Needle Threader

Mix and match! Using color is an easy way to grow your wardrobe exponentially. A black jacket goes with just about anything, as do black slacks. Black is beautiful and always so very elegant. Changing out the slacks for velvet burgundy bell bottoms brings a fresh, fun look. Just removing a jacket is an instant costume change.

If your masterpiece includes sewing heavy fabrics or leather, you will have to find some super-size needles and extra-strength thread. Be prepared for a more strenuous sewing session!

Enjoy all of the year-end festivities knowing the jingle in your pocket is the money you saved, and the complements you receive are a nod to *your* individual style and the couture that YOU created!

Just Be
YOU!

SLIP *in to Slinky*

Veronica was thrilled when she found an awesome red plaid jacket for $7.50. The only problem? Big, wide, green and yellow lapels…and it was a couple sizes too big!

Regardless, she absolutely loved the fabric and grabbed it off the rack with the hope of salvation. Then V found a lonely, studded (fake) leather jacket for $12.95. The poor coat was begging for a little TLC.

With a little snip and clip, joined with some clever handy-work, she built her own festive, elegant and original outfit. Total cost? Twenty bucks! Be creative. Have fun!

Slinky inner-ware (if you dare) keeps you warm and is perfect underneath any outfit. Veronica starts with a sleek, sexy black slip. This simple, yet elegant undergarment is acceptable attire for most Hollywood hot spots and (some) holiday cocktail parties. Comfortable and cool for late night dancing!

...P.M.

A Skank Is Born

Text: Bethany Taryeton

Meet Jessica Goodwin... Glam Skanks Drummer

When Glam Skanks were faced with the task of finding a drummer, they knew it could be a challenge. Technically known as a "Girl" band, the members are not concerned with gender, but instead are all about the music. They knew finding a good fit would be tough. However, the stars did their magic dance and helped talent find talent.

Introducing Glam Skanks awesome new drummer and truly brilliant human, *Jessica Goodwin*, the beautiful, bad-ass beat of the band! With a sparkling disposition and friendly confidence, Jess likes to hit um hard, creating a massive, heart-pounding array of punchy, powerful percussion. On stage, Jessica is magic in motion... grace, beauty and style... her bright eyes and contagious smile adding big fun to the show!

The first two performances with the all-new line up were House of Blues (Anaheim) and Novo Theater, Los Angeles; in support of the Adicts. The band has never sounded better, is booking next years' shows and can't wait to get back on the road. Please welcome Jessica via all Glam Skanks social media! Her solid playing can be heard on the much anticipated sophomore release by our beloved Glam Skanks. (Named Best Glitter Band by L.A. Weekly).

So much is happening that 2019 is already looking pretty crazy, starting the year off supporting the Dickies! Make sure not to miss Glam Skanks when they rock and roll through your town. Look for Jessica, the bright light in the back, the brains behind the beat, as the girls perform great new songs, as well as all of your favorites from "Glitter City".

Veronica, Millie and Vannessa are all so very excited to have Jessica join them on their super-sonic journey, criss-crossing the planet, meeting new people and performing in some of the most prestigious venues in the world. Welcome Jessica. It is an honor to have you on board!

Photo: David Kleeman

Jessica Goodwin

Favorite Color

"I don't have a favorite color, but most of my clothes are black."

Forest, Beach or Desert?

"All of the above! I love camping and hiking in the forest, visiting beaches all over the world, and I grew up in the desert."

Major Influences?

"Growing up, my favorite drummer was Adrian Young from the band No Doubt. I also really love John Bonham (doesn't every drummer??!) I am influenced by a lot of people, so I don't really like to call out names too much. I am influenced by my peers, by people I watch on line. There are so many incredible drummers out there."

Music that is must fun to play?

"Anything where I can go crazy and rock out. Usually something falling under the rock umbrella. That being said, I have played in different types of bands; and Glam Skanks of course!. I always have fun doing it!"

Favorite location you've ever been?

"A couple of my favorite places in the world are Nosara, Costa Rica and Tulum, Mexico. Also, I just spent a few weeks traveling Thailand, and that is high up on my list as well."

Dream location you want to visit?

"My dream is to see as much of the world as possible. So I want to go just about everywhere! I love going to other countries and experiencing different cultures.. I would really love to go on safari in Africa and explore Iceland. Those places are very high on my list."

First live performance?

"Middle school in concert band. I still remember we played "We Will Rock You"! Haha. My first show playing drum kit was with my high school punk band. We played in the parking lot of a Smoothie King in Vegas."

Most memorable live performance?

"I think I would say playing at the Hard Rock in Las Vegas. My parents were there, my aunt, uncle, cousin, best friend growing up (who I met in band class in 6th grade). My best friends parents and my girlfriend even drove from L.A. to come surprise me! I was coming through Vegas on tour with my old band, and I felt like that was the moment when I showed my parents that all of the hours they endured listening to me learn drums, and all of the money they spent getting me drum equipment and lessons, and driving me to rehearsals was not for nothing. It was really so special for me. I think only other time both of my parents have seen me perform was in middle school band. After I played we went to a restaurant in the Hard Rock and sat around and laughed. It was definitely one of those really special moments and my heart was filled with so much love and support."

Dream venue?

"Red Rocks Amphitheater in Colorado, and Radio City Music Hall in NYC!"

What do you want to be when you grow up?

"Happy and fulfilled. Aside from that, it would be amazing to be working in music full time."

Photos: Suzanne Allison

SPOT LIGHT

Glam Skanks lead vocalist Vannessa McNiel is so much more than a singer. Not only does she belt out the tunes with a gusto from deep within her soul, she also stomps the stage like a bad, bad bitch, ready to deal out a little karma if need be. With roots in Columbia and a huge heart of gold, this soft-spoken, kind earthling is funny, friendly and fabulous and entertains with a fierce, female presence...

It was a total fluke that lead vocalist Vannessa McNiel was tending bar at a swanky venue in downtown L.A., covering for a friend. She had never been there before that night. It was a holiday party for a bunch of over-dressed, nerdy theme park executives. With a bright, friendly smile and positive glow, she served a scotch to Glam Skanks tour manager. He asked if she had any life plans and she answered that she was a musician.

When he asked her what kind of music she was most passionate about, she answered with a gleam in her eye... "rock and roll". He handed her a download card of "Glitter City" the debut album by Glam Skanks. In return, she handed him a personalized guitar pick. The next morning, he searched, found and fell for the girl that would soon become the audio voice of Glam Skanks.

The rest is her story...

"I am a natural born explorer. I've been chasing around ideas on all aspects of life and stringing together melodies and words that mean something to me and to those who are listening. Since I can remember, I was always at my best when music was involved.

Whether I was dancing to it, writing it, or just listening; and no matter what it was, classic, rock, pop, oldies, Spanish, Cumbia, church gospels, whatever; you name it. I was into it all the way.

I am a lover! But I will fight for what I believe in. On stage I get to inspire so many women to be proud of their sexuality, and to own their talents and inspirations and build dreams with them.

I consider myself to be hyper and sometimes I can over-think things, but one thing is for sure, I am never bored. I love fronting Glam Skanks and I am grateful for every musical experience I have encountered on tour and at home."

Photos: Suzanne Allison

Backstage Rider

Photos: Len Scapoff

HIT OR MISS MEALS ON TH

Lovely Tradition Sunday Roast by Chef Wilf.

OAD.

When it comes to the Backstage Rider, (the snacks and drinks for the band and crew) Glam Skanks never know what they will find. More often than not, there is bottled water, beer, maybe a veggie plate or some potato chips. However, every once in awhile unexpected delicacies await!

Rib-Eye steak with the works at Brooklyn Bowl in Las Vegas, and Beyond burgers at House of Blues make up for the times when the fare doesn't seem fair at all!

Once at a beautiful, vintage, art deco theater in Canada, there was nothing! ...not even bottled water for the stage! No drink tickets for the band! Being a larger theater, the polite, black-suited bartenders were not allowed to give the band bottled water and the girls had to buy their own... at five bucks a bottle!

Now Glam Skanks are gracious young ladies and don't ask for a lot. As it turned out, the club's management was quite shocked to hear about it and the promoter was the one at fault. After the girls finished their set, the promoter brought them four (warm) water bottles. In return, she got an ear-full from the tour manager.

However, there are those times that the sweet starving Skanks are surprised to receive some palate pleasing perks in the sustenance department. Sometimes, as if a foodie dream come true, the girls are greeted with a fabulous feast.

When on a six-week UK tour supporting the one and only Adam Ant, Glam Skanks were fattened up by Adam's personal chef, "Wilf" and his pastry chef "Alice". Crazy-cuisine, every day, lunch and dinner! And breaking bread with Adam's band was always very special. Simply magical meals!

Fan Mail

We are always so proud and impressed when fans reach out and share their thoughts about our music. Our most sincere gratitude goes out to everyone that appreciates what we do. It's so awesome to know that our songs have a special meaning, have helped someone through tough times, or pumped up a party. Thanks again and again to all you Glam Skanks out there ... Much respect!

"Glam Skanks rock! I saw you last night and can't believe the awesome talent blasting off the stage. You really caught me off guard. No offense, but when a band of young girls totally out rock all the guys in the club, I bow down.
Jimmy... Reno, NV

"Thank you so much for a great show! Your song Anything In Between really meant a lot to me and my girlfriend. I am sixteen and it is great that you understand stuff."
Billie... Los Angeles, CA

"Thank you for one of the best shows I have ever seen. This was the third Glam Skanks show I saw and you just get better and better! Forever a fan!"
Gloria... New York, NY

"Dear Glam Skanks, Last night I dragged my grumpy twelve-year-old to see Adam Ant perform. I had no idea there was an opening band. You girls were absolutely fantastic! You were all so friendly after thee show, signed our cd and gave my kid a sticker and button. She couldn't believe she got to meet you "in person"! On the way home, she started writing lyrics and said that she starting a band. She told me her theme song is "Bad Bitch" and she woke up the next morning singing "Teenage Drag Queen". It's like she had brain surgery! Thank you for saving my daughter!"
Cherie... Dallas, TX

"Thank you for keeping great guitar rock alive!"
Dustin... Reno, NV

www.ingramcontent.com/pod-product-compliance
Lightning Source LLC
Chambersburg PA
CBHW040208240726
48664CB00002B/875